AF256150

MAGDALENE'S MEMOIRS

by Magdalene ('Mayleen') Zimmerling

ISBN 978-1-7774324-2-3

All photos from family sources.

Cover and interior design by Saw-mon and Natalie Design.

Map by Jitan Dahal.

Published by NextGen Story: Custom Publishing
www.nextgenstory.com

PREFACE

Magdalene (Mayleen) is one of the strongest and bravest people I have ever known. I imagine myself in her stories of our ancestors, as early settlers with dreams of a better life, consumed by their work to carve out an existence and survive the harsh Canadian landscape. I doubt I would have fared as well as she did.

In these chapters you will learn about Ruth and Donny's heartbreaking deaths. I remember hearing Ruth's story when I was a child and it instilled in me a deep appreciation for universal health care. The idea that access to medical care should be based on need, not ability to pay, is now a defining Canadian value that must be protected. Donny and Ruth's premature deaths remind us of the tragic consequences if we fail to do so. To this day, their stories ground my work in medical education.

Despite many barriers and a lack of formal education, Magdalene persevered. In the face of hardship, adversity, and tragedy, Magdalene showed courage and resourcefulness to make her own way in the world when others had different plans for her.

On her 95th birthday, I wanted to honour her extraordinary resilience with a book that captures some of her stories for future generations. It is my hope that Magdalene's memoirs will serve to remind us of our family's humble beginnings, help us recognize the privilege we've acquired from the sacrifices and difficult decisions made by those who came before us, and inspire us in difficult times. It is especially for our girls – may they have the strength and courage to challenge the systems, structures, and social norms that constrain their dreams and desires – just as Magdalene did.

– Cathy, Magdalene's granddaughter

Map of Otter lake and area

Route 301
Range Lake Cabin
Zimmerling Farm
Lac du Rang
Otter Lake Town
L. Mistassi
L. Abitibi
QUÉBEC
Rs. Gouin
Dozois Res.
Cabonga Res.
L. Kipawa
Rs. Baskatong
Sudbury
L. Nipissing
ONTARIO
Otter Lake Town
Shawville
Ottawa
L. Huron Georgian Bay
Montréal
L. Simcoe
Big Rideau L.
L. Champla
N
W
E
S
0 25 50 100
Kilometers
UNITED STATES
L. Ontario
5

BABY MAYLEEN

I was born July 18, 1926. I was baptized Magdalene Bertha Elizabeth.

When I was little, I couldn't say Magdalene. I called myself "Mawleen" which became Mayleen. Everyone around Otter Lake knew me as Mayleen.

We lived in a two-room log cabin with a built-on summer kitchen. My father cut the cedar shakes for the roof. We all slept in the one room upstairs with no partitions to separate one from the other. There were two handmade, wooden beds, with straw mattresses, one for my mother and father and one for two children, with a third, narrow cot for the third child. There was a table which held stacks of clothing and a second table Minnie (my mother) used for her sewing. Clothing was hung on racks. I think my brother Donny slept downstairs on a couch. I do not know how my mother was able to raise four children in such cramped quarters.

Downstairs was a leather foldout couch, a cot, a large table, a long bench, some chairs, a couple of built-in cupboards, an icebox, and the stove which served for all the heating and cooking, and a wash stand with a cupboard under it. There wasn't room for a wood-box, so the wood was piled behind or under the stove.

There were only two small windows, but they were very deep. In the spring my mother would sow tomato seeds in tin cans and these were kept in these windows and in the windows upstairs.

The walls of the house, being built of whole logs, were very thick. The cracks were chinked with a lime plaster and whitewashed with a lime wash. I remember eating bits of the lime plaster – maybe it was a good source of calcium!

Under the floor, reached by a trapdoor, was a root cellar. Here was stored (in sand) a vast quantity of potatoes, turnips, and carrots. Potatoes were kept for months in a simple hole dug into the ground and covered with straw. The summer kitchen was used during the hot weather for all the cooking, baking, and canning. In the winter it was used for storage. A few times family members also stayed there.

We had no electricity and no telephone. I was twelve before we even had a radio, and that was given to us by a man who owned a cottage on the lake.

One of my favorite places was a stream that cut through the fields, on its way to the lake. I spent many happy hours there with my imaginary friends, or just dreaming my childish dreams. There were huge, purple violets growing amongst the ferns along the banks. The stream was inhabited by large bullfrogs and many little fish. My father made a fish trap by fastening a piece of heavy wire around the opening of a burlap sack. I would then wedge this trap at a point in the stream, go up-stream and with a stick, I would poke and thrash the water to drive the fish down-stream into the sack. If I caught anything large enough, it was taken home for dinner. The rest were released back into the stream.

Minnie with me as a baby

House, Barns, and landscape

DAILY LIFE

There was no running water, not even a pump. I don't know why they never installed one! All the water used had to be carried in buckets from a natural spring several hundred feet from the house. In the summer, it was my chore to carry buckets of water for the garden. Occasionally, a small animal would succeed in drowning itself in the well and then my father would have to empty the well and clean it out. Quite a chore!

A bucket of water was kept on the washstand, with a dipper. Everyone drank from the same dipper. Another dipper was hanging on a tree branch by the well, good for an icy, cold drink.

Saturday night was bath night. A large, copper boiler was kept filled with water on the stove. A wash tub was placed beside the stove, water was then dipped from the boiler and everyone took a turn in the tub. If we were going to church the next day, our hair would be washed as well, and my mother would put our hair up in rag curlers, so that our hair would be in ringlets.

Minnie and me as a toddler

Otherwise, our hair was washed on Sunday and braided into pigtails which had to last all week.

There was no indoor plumbing, and everyone had outhouses. For toilet paper, the previous years' Simpson's and Eaton's catalogues came in handy. My mother only dealt with Eaton's, but the pictures in the Simpson's catalogues were far more colorful. When I found the Simpson's in someone else's outhouse I wanted to rip some out to make paper dolls. My mother wouldn't let me. she said it was stealing.

SEASONS ON THE FARM

Summer

During the summer there was always a lot of canning and preserving to be done. We would 'put down' the fruits as they ripened, and the vegetables.

My mother would send me out to the fields to pick wild strawberries. Sometimes Esther would come with me. I loved those times. I loved the heat of the sun, the fragrance of the hay and the daisies, the sound of grasshoppers and robins.

We would also make a day of picking blueberries. We had to go farther afield for that, and it was not so much fun. My mother was there, and she kept us picking!

Cranberries and choke cherries were gathered for jelly. They were cooked and placed in a sugar sack and hung over a pot to drain, and the syrup was then made into jelly.

My mother made dill pickles by layering them in barrels with cherry leaves and brine. I was sent to gather the cherry leaves. The leaves added a unique flavor to the pickles, a flavor I have never tasted since.

Spring

There were quite a few maple trees on the hill above the farm. In the spring my father would bore holes and set taps in these trees. Buckets were hung to catch the sap, which was then boiled into syrup. A very large bucket of sap was required to make a pint of syrup.

In the spring the days were warm and sunny, the snow would melt and overnight it would freeze into a hard crust, easy to walk upon. The snow was deep enough to completely cover the fences, about three and a half feet. We were able to take our sleds and go for very long rides down the hills and over the fields.

At Easter, the Easter bunny came and left hard boiled colored eggs in the hats we had left out on the veranda. My mother used onion peel for yellow, beet juice for red and pink, and she also had some food coloring that she used.

Fall/Winter

We didn't celebrate Halloween. There was no trick or treating.

Winter was the time my mother would make quilts and knit all the socks, mittens, toques, and scarves. The children wore long, rough, woolen stockings. I remember how they would itch, and they would take forever to dry.

The log cabin in winter

MEALS

I don't remember ever going hungry, although I know at times meals were pretty meager. There were no soft drinks, potato chips, or other goodies.

Breakfast was porridge, boiled eggs and toast. The oatmeal was purchased in large bags. My mother made her own "Red River" cereal. My sister Esther and I would have to do the grinding. We would grind wheat, buckwheat and barley in the meat grinder.

The main meal was served in the middle of the day: usually boiled potatoes with gravy, one or two vegetables and meat. For meat, most often we would have boiled beef, roasted pork, or slices of bologna. Sometimes there would be partridge or boiled venison, and on special occasions we'd have roasted chicken. In the winter my father and I went ice fishing, and there would be fish.

We never had salads, but in the spring, my mother would gather the leaves of lamb's quarters, a spinach-like plant that grew wild. Instead of serving this as a salad, it was cooked and served with butter.

For supper we had fried potatoes, meat sometimes if my father was working hard, molasses on bread, fruit, and puddings. My favorite was thick cream on bread, with brown sugar.

One winter, when my father was away at a logging camp, we had only potatoes, bread, and gravy. My mother made the gravy by browning flour and adding a bit of grease.

I remember that was the spring my mother killed the groundhog. We hadn't had any meat for weeks. The groundhog had a burrow in the orchard. My mother set a fire at one end of the burrow to chase the groundhog out. She waited at the other end and hit it with a stick, but she missed and only stunned it.

I don't believe she intended me to see any of this. She had sent me off on an errand, but I came back too soon, to find her beating the groundhog to death. She had injured it and had to finish the job. The little creature was putting up such a brave fight. I remember running, with the tears streaming down my face, begging her to stop.

We had meat for supper that day, but I refused to eat any. My mother didn't insist. She understood.

Woodstove where all the cooking happened

OUTINGS TO OTTER LAKE - AND CAMPING

During those early years my father didn't have a car, and so travel was done by horse and wagon or by sleigh depending on the season. There weren't too many fun outings.

It was about four or five miles to my grandparents' place. Otter Lake was seven miles away and Shawville was twenty five.

When my father went to Otter Lake to shop, he would always bring us a small bag of mixed or peppermint candy. Sometimes it would be long, slender tubes of candied popcorn, with a prize inside. They cost two cents each.

I especially remember one outing we had. My mother took us to the Shawville fair, which was held every fall. There was a parade and a carousel with its exciting music. There were so many different displays of quilts, pickles, jams, and baked goods, and an assortment of farm animals. We brought our own bagged lunch, but we were allowed to buy an ice cream cone.

One outing we always looked forward to was an overnight camping trip to Range Lake to fish for trout. Two or three times each spring when fishing season opened, we would finish the milking early and load the wagon with food and blankets. There would usually be other neighbors as well, scattered round the lake, each smug in the assumption he had the best fishing spot.

For the children there were wildflowers and wintergreen berries and wood to be gathered for the bonfires. For supper there were sandwiches, and tea steeped over the fire.

The men fished all night. The children would go to sleep, wrapped in blankets around the fire, with the stars overhead, the flickering campfires all around the lake, and the sound of the men calling back and forth, asking if the fish were biting in their spot.

In the morning we would awaken to the smell of coffee perking and fish frying over the fire.

Me as a young girl, playing outside

SPECIAL OCCASIONS

Weddings

Whenever there was a wedding, the celebration would begin in the afternoon, after the ceremony, and carry on until the wee hours of the morning. There would be an early supper, which was more like a feast with so many different dishes, pie, cake, and cookies.

The men would return home to their respective farms to take care of chores, and come back to take part in the square and round dancing. A lot of "moonshine" was 'secretly' consumed, so the wives wouldn't know. This stuff was like poison, and my father really couldn't handle it like some of the men. But he could never refuse, and always became deathly sick after.

There were two or three fiddlers and a caller or two. The dance floor was in a barn, if there was space, or a platform would have been erected, out under the stars. I'm not sure what they would have done if it had been raining. There were benches around the dance floor for the elderly and mothers with babies and children. Babies and very young children were wrapped in blankets and slept on the benches throughout the music and shouting. The older children ran around and played in the exciting darkness. At midnight, more food was served: sandwiches, salmon, bologna, and egg salad, along with more cake and cookies, coffee, and tea.

Christmas

Christmas was a special time. We looked forward to it for months. Much time was spent going through the Eaton's catalogue, choosing what we wanted Santa to bring. We always had a tree, with a star on top. (I don't remember how we found space for the tree!)

About a week or so before Christmas, my father would stay up late making cedar garlands and hanging them from corner to corner on the ceiling, with red bells. When we awakened in the morning we could smell the fragrance of the cedar. My father said Santa came during the night and hung them.

We didn't get much for Christmas. There were always oranges, and that was the only time we had them! We would get a bag of mixed nuts, a bag of peanuts in the shell, and a bag of mixed candy. There would be a scribbler or two, a package of crayons or a box of paints. One Christmas I was given a little blue tin tea set with tiny forks, knives and spoons. Another time I got a set of aluminum pots and pans. Ruth always got paints and drawing paper. I remember she spent a lot of time painting.

I don't remember what the main course was for Christmas dinner, I think roast chicken. My mother made 'kuchen' which is a type of loaf filled with raisins and iced with frosting, cookies, and an apple or raisin pie.

Ruth and I dressed up for a special occasion

MY MOTHER: MINNIE

Minnie, my mother, was 14 years old when she was sent to Montreal to work as a maid for a family called the Hollands. Part of her salary was sent home to help her family. Minnie had never been away from her family before, or so far from home. Everything was so different from what she had been used to. She was very lonely and homesick. Minnie worked at this same place for four years.

She became involved with a young man, probably a friend of the Hollands. She said they were in love and wanted to get married, but the young man's mother didn't want him to have anything to do with Minnie. He was also suffering from tuberculosis and died without ever knowing Minnie was pregnant with his child. Minnie didn't let his mother know she was pregnant, for fear the mother would take her baby from her. Minnie was forced to give up her job and return home to have her baby in shame and disgrace. She always felt she had failed her father and disgraced him.

I think she always felt a bit ashamed of everything back in those days. In those days an unwed mother was looked down on and shamed: it was her fault, the woman's fault, not the man's fault. I think she probably felt that she wanted to withdraw from everything.

My mother named her son Daniel, but she always called him Donny. Perhaps that was Daniel's father's name. When Daniel was two years old, Minnie married my father, Charles Zimmerling. They were second cousins. She wanted to give Daniel a home and a father.

Minnie was a beautiful woman, with brown hair and grey eyes. She could be gentle and kind. When her sisters needed help, in any way, she was there for them.

When my Uncle Russell left Aunt Amelia Cobb with two small children, Minnie stepped in and brought her and the children to live in the summer kitchen for the winter, which gave Amelia time to assess her situation and make plans for herself and her children.

Aunt Martha lived on the other side of the lake behind us and over the hill. She had many problems, as well as many babies. Whenever she had another baby, Minnie would be over there, helping. Many times Aunt Martha would bring her little children and spend the night with us, so she could lay all her problems at Minnie's feet. Even though Minnie had very little herself, she would give Martha clothing and food.

But Minnie was also a very strong and domineering person. She was very determined about the kind of farm she wanted to build. She simply couldn't see that we couldn't make a decent living on the farm. My mother was a very strong willed, determined person. I think I take after her more than I do my dad.

"Minnie and her boy", Donny

Minnie ? and her boy 1916

MINNIE AND CHARLES

Charles had lost his mother, Bertha, when he was just a baby. His father married Elizabeth when Charles was about 10, and they had three more children; Annie, Lena, and John. When Charles was about fifteen and his father was away from home one cold, winter's night, their house caught fire and burned. Elizabeth told Charles to stay with the little children while she walked out to the neighbors for help. She didn't make it. Her body was later found, frozen about half way to the neighbors. This was during the winter of 1916. The three younger children were taken in and raised by friends, Charles remained with his father.

Charles was illiterate, but he was kind, gentle, honest and generous, always laughing, always cheerful. Everyone who knew him loved and respected him. He loved Minnie and adored his children. He had no special skills. He was an adventurer and enjoyed working with other people.

For the first few years my mother followed him from job to job, working in logging camps, harvesting on the prairies, etc. He probably would have eventually settled down in a permanent job somewhere.

Minnie wasn't happy with this lifestyle. She wanted to put down roots. She persuaded Charles to move back to the property owned by his father and start farming. Charles hated farming. He was not, and would never be a farmer. But he loved Minnie and could never say no to her. Because there was never enough money realized from the farm, he still had to work in logging camps during the winters.

Although I know my parents loved us and I wouldn't call it a cold environment, there were no demonstrations of love or affection. My mother was very critical of my father, and of me, because, she said, I was very like my father. I don't believe my mother loved my father. Hers was a marriage of convenience, for Donny.

ROUNDING UP THE CATTLE

My parents kept chickens and pigs, and Minnie grew a large vegetable garden along with potatoes and turnips. Eggs from the chickens and butter from the cows was traded for other goods at the General Store in Otter Lake. My mother sold Watkins products to augment the family income.

Minnie gradually built up a small herd of milk cows. We didn't have enough pasture land to graze the cattle, so every morning they were turned out to wander and forage in the hills. In the evening, my father would have to walk miles sometimes to find the cattle and bring them home for milking. They were kept in a small pasture overnight and turned out again the next morning.

When I was old enough, it became my chore to round them up. One summer evening it was raining, and because of the rain, difficult to hear the cowbells. I thought I heard them up on the hill behind the farm, but I became turned around and was no longer certain in which direction I was going. Because of the clouds I couldn't check directions by the sun.

It was growing dark. I couldn't hear anything because of the noise of rain on the leaves. On one side of our farm was the hill, on the other side, a lake. If I chose the wrong direction, I could walk for miles and just get deeper and deeper into forest.

Fortunately, I chose the right direction, and came to a fence between us and our neighbor, so I knew where I was.

When I arrived home, I found my father had found the cattle and brought them home, and was out looking for me. I had been gone for quite some time.

When a Creamery opened in Shawville, my mother bought a cream separator so we could sell the cream. The cream separator was a complicated piece of equipment. There were some thirty stainless steel, cone shaped discs along with a few other pieces. Twice each day, after the milk had been put through, all these parts had to be taken apart and thoroughly washed and scalded and put back together again. The discs had to be put together in a certain order or the machine wouldn't work. When we obtained this machine, I was old enough to take over this chore. Heaven help me if I got the discs out of order!!

The Creamery sent a truck around once a week to pick up the cream from the farmers. The truck wouldn't come in to our farm. My father had to take the cream cans out to the neighbors. The cream was kept from spoiling by keeping them lowered in the icy spring waters. Those cream cheques coming in must have been a God-send.

Minnie with a dairy cow and bucket for milking

FARM LIFE: GRAIN, PARTRIDGE, AND LIME

Minnie had grand dreams of the farm and house she would have one day. I remember her talking about her plans. She was very stubborn. She could not seem to see that a financially viable farm was not possible there. Even as a young teenager, I could see that we didn't have the acreage to grow enough food for the cattle that she wanted to have. There were hills on one side and a lake on the other. I'm not like my mother in that way – I can accept what's possible and what isn't possible.

When the grain was harvested, a threshing machine that went from farm to farm would come in and thresh the wheat, oats, barley and buckwheat. This usually took several hours, which meant preparing two or three meals for the half dozen or so men. Sometimes they had to remain overnight. The children weren't allowed near the machinery, but this was an exciting event, and I would get as close as I could to watch the sheaves of grain being fed into the hungry jaws and the golden grain pouring out into sacks held by the men.

When Charles was at home and when Donny was old enough, trapping for fur pelts was done as well. When I was about thirteen, my father taught me how to handle a small .22 rifle. I practiced by shooting at marked tin cans on a fence post. My aim became quite accurate and my father took me with him one day to hunt partridge, but I found I couldn't shoot them. I never went hunting with him again.

My father built a lime kiln into the side of a hill. The place was littered with pink/white limestone. This was gathered and hauled to the kiln. A very hot fire had to be kept burning for several hours to melt the limestone. My father would stay up all night and keep the fire roaring. When the limestone had melted and cooled down, it was stored in a deep pit until being used or sold. Lime wash was used instead of paint on the inside of buildings.

When a sawmill was built in Otter Lake, my father would cut logs in the winter, haul them to Otter Lake and sell them to the mill. The trip to Otter Lake was seven miles by horse and sleigh.

Those years must have been difficult. The winters were cold and harsh. The summers were often hot and humid, with endless mosquitoes and blackflies.

My mother and the whole family would have had a much better and easier life if she had allowed my father to work at the mill and been willing to live in Otter Lake, which he wanted.

Charles and Minnie working on the farm

SCHOOL

My mother decided we didn't need to attend school. Attending school wasn't compulsory at that time, and I guess her reasons were valid. The school was a good four miles from where we lived, and part of the trek was a lonely one. The school was also closed during the worst part of the winter, and I have my doubts about the quality of the education the children received. I do believe that the social interaction benefits for the children would have outweighed the "reading, writing and 'rithmetic".

A few first grade primers had been obtained from someone, and my mother taught us to read from those. She also had basic arithmetic, which she taught us. History and geography weren't included.

Reading material was almost non-existent. We subscribed to a weekly newspaper, The Family Herald and Weekly Star. Of course, there was the Bible. A cousin, who was a member of the Pentecostal church, would save all the Sunday School papers for us, and my two younger aunts, Rosie and Ellie would give my mother all the trashy romance magazines they read: True Story, True Romance, and others. This was my reading material! I grew up with a very warped view of love and romance.

One year when I was about seven, my mother, for some reason, wanted me to take part in the school concert. I believe it had something to do with my mother and my Aunt Amelia, each wanting to prove their child was the smartest and prettiest.

My cousin Elizabeth was two months older than me. I was supposed to do "Little Brown Jug" in the concert. For weeks I practiced my piece, so it would be perfect. My mother made me a very pretty brown velvet dress for the occasion.

When the name of the piece was announced, I jumped up to run to the stage, when my mother was told my cousin Myrna was doing that piece. I had to quickly choose another little song to do. The only other one I knew really well was "Jesus Loves Me".

I went up on stage and did my song, but it just wasn't as neat as "Little Brown Jug".
And then Santa arrived with a loud "Ho, Ho, Ho", and a big bag on his back. Everyone was called up and got to sit on his lap and receive a small gift and a bag of candy.

Me as a young girl

PLAYMATES

I had no playmates and never had any friends. We had no toys, no games and no books.

My sister, Esther, was three years younger than myself, and a rather withdrawn child. Esther was a follower and I was a leader, so Esther did whatever I told her to do in the games we played. We played a lot of games, all make-believe games. I made them up.

My mother was very distressed when she learned she was pregnant with Esther. She did not want another child, and even tried to end the pregnancy. My mother felt this was the reason Esther was so quiet and withdrawn, and slow to develop. Also, because she felt guilty, she became over-protective of Esther, and further hampered Esther's development by constantly telling us (and Esther) that she was "different" and shouldn't be expected to do and learn like other children.

My mother kept Esther very close to home. She was treated differently and had everything done for her, consequently, she developed into a very selfish and self-centered person. So mostly, I was on my own.

Aunt Amelia, my mother's sister, felt more like a mother to me than my own mother. She was more understanding. My mother, for instance, didn't want me to know where babies came from, right up until I was beginning menstruation. She didn't succeed in that because Aunt Amelia was more forthright with her daughter. And Elizabeth, of course, told me everything.

Aunt Amelia was my hero. She was my favorite relative, along with Elizabeth, my cousin.

In the 30s during the Great Depression, Uncle Russell couldn't find work and so he left Aunt Amelia to go look for work. He ended up joining the army because that meant that he could send a cheque home to them. That first winter they were renting a house, and they had no place to go. They came to stay with us. I remember my father taking me with him when we went with the horse and wagon to bring them and their little bits of furniture back to our place.

They spent the winter in our summer kitchen, which had a couple of cots in it. My dad put a heater in for them, and they lived there for that winter. And then in the spring, my aunt borrowed money from her brother. They had a house built on a piece of property at the back, it was a beautiful place. She lived there for the rest of her life until she died.

Esther and my father with hay bales

READING IN FRONT OF THE FIRE

Because coal oil for the lamps was scarce and expensive, we had to use the light from the fire as much as possible. I would sit, reading, in front of the fire, which was probably just as bright as the oil lamps. Many times my mother would be angry with me when she caught me reading instead of doing the chores I had been assigned.

The Hollands, the people my mother had worked for in Montreal, would periodically send boxes of used clothing. One time they sent a box of children's books - hard cover! My joy knew no bounds. There were some Hardy Boys books in there, and Girl Scouts of America books. There was a series called "Mother West Winds Children", and a few others as well.

That box of books was so very important, as we didn't have books, we didn't have anything. One that I especially loved was "A Child's Garden of Verses" by Robert Lewis Stevenson. I would lose myself in the poems. It gave me a glimpse into a world that I didn't know. I remember reading one about a child who was saying he was sick upon his bed. He had his little toy soldiers, and he played with them. They played in his counterpane, and I remember thinking 'counterpane' - that was a new word for me. A totally different word, meaning blankets, quilts, and so on. It was just so neat. I still love that book.

My mother had a large trunk in which she kept all her more precious things. I only remember the beautiful, pop-out greeting cards, a tiny china tea set and a doll that belonged to my sister Ruth. We were never allowed to play with these.

Each child had its own special place to keep their treasures. My sister Ruth had a large wooden box in which she kept her paints and papers. I had a flat trunk, which could be stored under a bed. I don't remember everything I had stored in it, pieces of embroidery, scrapbooks, my doll and doll's clothes I had made, a water color set, crayons, my paper dolls. The trunk had been moved to the new house and was destroyed in the fire.

When I was sick and lay a-bed,
I had two pillows at my head,
And all my toys beside me lay,
To keep me happy all the day.
And sometimes for an hour or so
I watched my leaden soldiers go,
With different uniforms and drills,
Among the bed-clothes, through the hills;
And sometimes sent my ships in fleets
All up and down among the sheets;
Or brought my trees and houses out,
And planted cities all about.
I was the giant great and still
That sits upon the pillow-hill,
And sees before him, dale and plain,
The pleasant land of counterpane.

- Robert Lewis Stevenson

R. L. Stevenson, "Child's Garden of Verses"

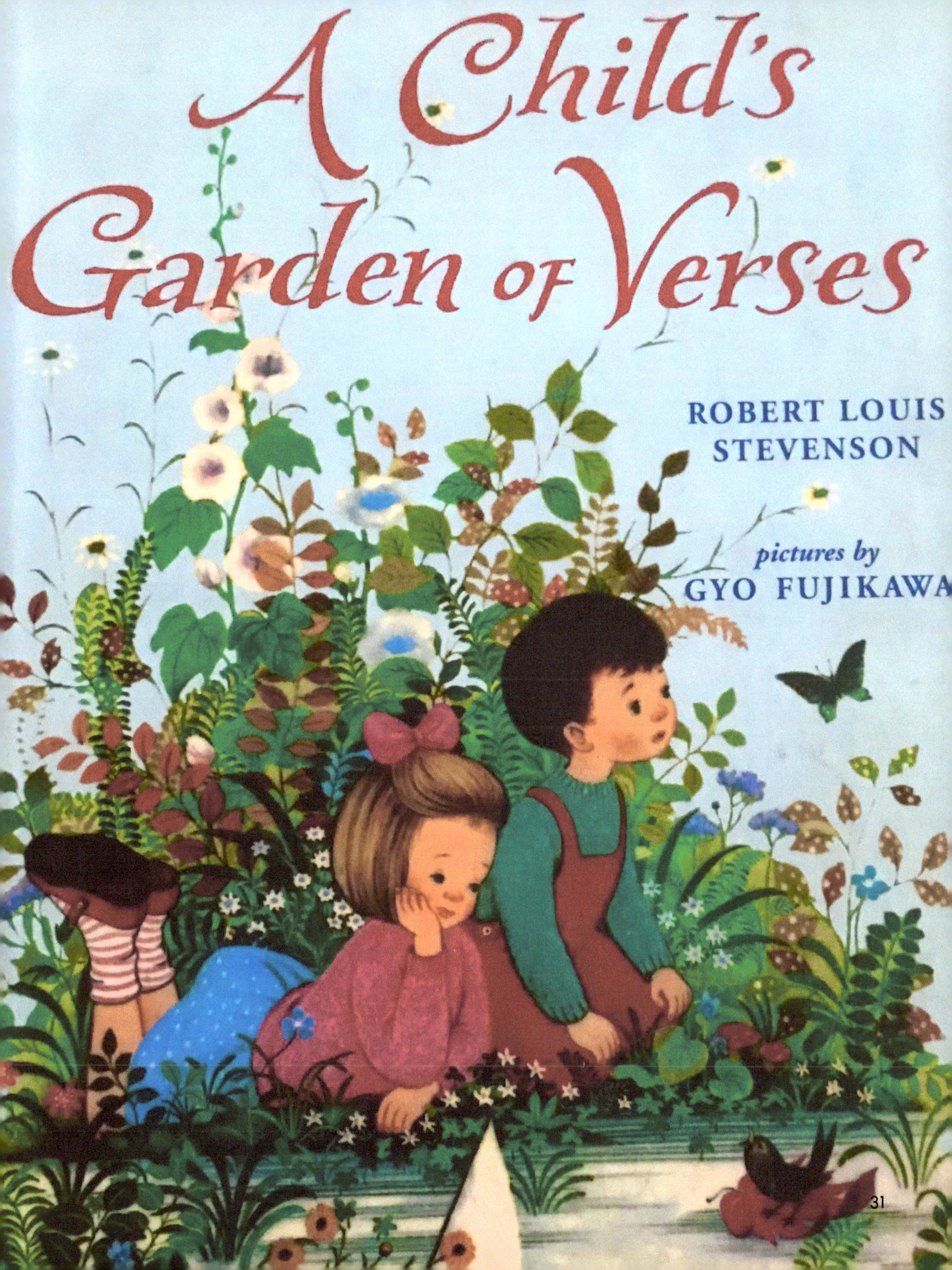
A Child's
Garden of Verses
ROBERT LOUIS
STEVENSON
pictures by
GYO FUJIKAWA

DONNY

In April of 1935, when I was eight and a half, my twenty one year old brother, Donny became ill and died. It was in the spring, and he had been in the bush, working for one of my uncles. Someone brought a message that he was very ill, and that my father should come bring him home.

He had pneumonia. Ruth, Esther and I had to sleep on mats downstairs, so Donny could have a bed upstairs. I guess my mother didn't realize how ill Donny really was. The nearest doctor was in Shawville and I doubt he would have come anyway. There were no antibiotics back then.

My mother was upstairs with Donny. It was very warm in the house, and she had the upstairs windows open for fresh air. I heard her cry out, "Donny, Donny, don't leave, come back!" In my child's mind, a vision sprang up of Donny flying out through the window!

My mother came running downstairs, crying, telling me to hurry, get dressed, and get help from the neighbors. I ran all the way. The road was deep in mud and slush, and by the time I reached our neighbor my feet were soaked and I was almost sick myself.

The neighbor brought me back with horse and sleigh, but of course there was nothing anyone could do. I remember being huddled in a corner by the stove when they brought the body down to place him in the summer kitchen. My mother had to wash and dress the body. Someone had a casket built and it was brought in.

I don't remember the funeral. No one thought of the children. Nothing was explained. Ruth was fourteen, and I guess she had to take over the meals and see to the little ones.

I have only a couple of vague memories of my older brother. Donny was twelve years older than me. I was about three or four, dressed for the outdoors on a cold winter's day. I was outside with Donny. He decided to check his trap line and he thought my mother was watching me. She thought Donny was. I tried to follow Donny, but the snow was too deep for my short legs. Fortunately, Donny wasn't gone too long. He found me on the trail, in the snow. My mittens were gone and my hands were nearly frozen. I remember him picking me up and carrying me home and my mother rubbing my hands with snow.

My mother took Donny's death very hard. He had been her child and hers alone, and I guess her favorite.

Daniel "Donny" Zimmerling

RUTH

The following year, June 1936, Ruth became ill with pains in her side. She was fifteeen years old.

My father still didn't own a car, so once again I was sent out to the neighbors to find someone to drive Ruth and my mother to the doctor in Shawville. This Doctor was known to frequently be under the influence of alcohol, but he was the only Doctor available. He examined Ruth and told my mother to take her home, and if the pain persisted to bring her back.

Two days later, Ruth was in agony. This time my father went out to find someone to drive them to Shawville. The Doctor's diagnosis this time was acute appendicitis. Shawville didn't have a hospital at this time, so Ruth was taken to Ottawa. The hospital there refused to accept her, because my mother hadn't come prepared to pay up front the fee required.

Ruth had to be driven all the way to Montreal, over roads that were not in the good condition they are today. When she arrived at the Montreal hospital, the appendix had burst, spreading the toxins throughout her system. She was in the hospital for at least two weeks, fighting for her life.

I remember there was time enough for my mother to send a parcel to us with a pretty cotton dress and bloomers for each of us.

The annual school picnic was being held at this time, and my Aunt Amelia suggested my father bring Esther and me to the picnic. We wore our new dresses, and I joined in all the races and games, but Esther was too shy to participate. It was such a fun day, and my father was enjoying himself as well, chatting with all the other parents. We had no way to know how sadly our day was to end.

On our way home, as we were passing our neighbor's place, Olga was waiting for us with the sad news that Ruth had died. My mother was bringing her body home by train. Arrangements had to be made for them to be picked up at the station in Shawville and brought to our house.

The funeral arrangements had to be made very quickly. This was summer, and the weather was very warm. I remember the casket being carried from the house and my mother taking pictures of Ruth in the casket. Several of my mother's sisters were elected to be pall bearers. I remember nothing of the funeral itself.

Ruth Zimmerling

RUTH'S PLAYHOUSE

My sister Ruth was five years older than me. My father built Ruth a playhouse. It was situated in a small grove of trees in the cattle pasture, quite some way from the house. For some unknown reason, Ruth would never play with me or let me play in her playhouse. It had a window, with little curtains and some wooden crates for table and chairs.

I had an imaginary house in a pile of boulders not too far from her playhouse. I remember having imaginary friends, particularly since I had no real friends. They were all girls, the imaginary girls that I played with and did things with. I assembled a tiny tea set from acorn caps and flat smooth rocks and had tea parties with my imaginary friends.

I was nine when Ruth died. The summer after her death I asked if I could use her playhouse. My mother refused, saying it had belonged to Ruth and no one was going to use it. This was one of the few times my father stood up to my mother. He said he had built the playhouse for Ruth, and now he was giving it to me.

I remember Ruth made me a rag doll. It had yellow yarn for hair, buttons for eyes and a painted mouth. She made some clothes for the doll. I loved that doll and I named her Bon-Amie.

Sadly, Bon-Amie came to a very abrupt end one summer's day. Some boys were visiting and threw Bon-Amie over the house. We couldn't find her anywhere. One of the boys must have chucked her under the rose bushes because we couldn't find her. In the fall, when the leaves were off the bushes, she was found under a bush, muddy and dirty with her face washed off. Despite my tears, my mother said she was beyond salvaging and threw her in the fire. I was devastated – I'd found Bon-Amie, and now she was gone again.

That Christmas, Santa brought me a new doll. But it couldn't replace Bon-Amie!

TOUGH YEARS: MY MOTHER GRIEVING

My mother must have nearly lost her mind. She was still grieving over the loss of Donny, and now Ruth was gone too. A few weeks after the funeral, we received back the pictures my mother had taken of Ruth in the casket. I withdrew and didn't want to look at them. My mother was clutching Esther to her and crying and calling out "Why, why did it have to be Ruth, my beautiful Ruth, why did God take her?" In my mind I felt she was wishing it could have been me instead of Ruth, because I felt I was too tall and skinny and not very pretty. Esther was still cute and cuddly and received hugs and attention. I was never hugged.

Minnie withdrew from all of us, neglecting her remaining children, the house, and the garden. She would be gone for hours, walking the fields and hills. When I was older, she told me how angry she had been with God for taking her beloved children. Asking what she had done to deserve being punished like this. She was certain it was her fault, something she had done.

She had no one to talk to. We were very isolated from family and friends. The minister of our church lived away from Otter Lake and had several parishes to attend to, and anyway, one was supposed to take a death in stride and not fall apart like that. There were no counsellors, and I gather her sisters were not there for her either. I was too young to understand what was happening. Her behavior frightened me, and I guess it affected Esther as well.

My mother remained like that throughout the summer. She wouldn't go to visit anywhere, not even to church. A couple of times when we went to Otter Lake to shop, we would visit the graves of Ruth and Donny, and she would fall apart all over again. My father did his best to cope, but he was grieving too. I remember how sad he was. He didn't laugh anymore.

I was ten, and I had to muddle through cooking meals and taking care of Esther. I even had to help milk the cows. It was frightening for Esther and me. I know I felt I had lost my mother. She was a stranger, I couldn't understand her behavior. She would be angry with me for no reason at all. It seemed that nothing I did was right. One time I overheard her say to my father about some issue, that it "probably was old skinny long-legs" referring to me.

Winter was upon us, and we were more isolated than ever. I think she wanted to keep us isolated from the rest of the world. Maybe she thought she was keeping us safe, Esther and me. My mother became even more silent and withdrawn. My father, because he didn't know what to do, became very quiet also.

I began to have nightmares, and then my mind fixated on the notion that my parents wanted to kill me. I don't remember how long this phase lasted. I would force myself to stay awake at night, lying in terror, waiting for them to come up. Of course I would fall asleep anyway. I began to stammer, which lasted for years.

MONTREAL APPLE AND APPENDICITIS

When I was ten, my mother took Esther and me to Montreal to have our tonsils removed. We stayed with a cousin of hers. We were still recovering from whooping cough so the doctor refused to operate, and we had to wait a week.

One day while shopping at a market I was checking all the barrels of dill pickles, herring, and cookies. One barrel had beautiful red, shining apples. I was wearing a coat with deep pockets. Before I even realized what I was doing, one of those apples was in my pocket.

When we left the store, I showed my mother the apple. She was horrified, but she didn't make me return it. Instead she said I was very wicked, and that God would punish me for my sin of stealing.

That winter, I was playing near the wood stove and fell with my right hand on the hot stove. It was quite badly burned. My mother's reaction was, "I told you God would punish you." That night I couldn't sleep, I was in such pain. My father sat beside me for hours, fanning my hand with a magazine.

That spring, I came down with appendicitis. When I began complaining of pain in my side, my mother rushed me to a Doctor in Campbell's Bay. My father had by this time acquired a used car. I was diagnosed with acute appendicitis and taken to the hospital in Shawville. This hospital had only been open a few months. It was set up in a large, old house.

This incident with me frightened my mother badly. She said she felt God was taking her children, one by one. It served to bring her out of the depression she was in.

That year on my eleventh birthday, she gave a birthday party for me.

Me at age 11 or so on Tess

39

My eleventh birthday celebration

MY ELEVENTH BIRTHDAY

We always had a cake on our birthday. It was frosted and decorated, but I don't remember candles, and of course, there were no gifts.

My mother gave a special birthday party for me on my eleventh birthday. I think my cousin Elizabeth had had one sometime and I said that I would like to have one.

All the aunts, uncles and cousins came. My grandfather was there as well. We actually had party hats! This time my cake had pink candles, with little rosette candle holders. I remember there were no presents but some of the people gave me $1 or 50 cents.

The daughter of a man who owned a cottage on Range Lake was invited. She was about two years older than me. Her gift was a dress that was too small for her. It was pale green, soft and silky, with ruffles and lace. I thought it the most beautiful dress I had ever seen. I think I wore it at the party. I put it on to wear it because I didn't have anything really nice

myself.

Although my mother had invited all these people for my party, it sort of died there - once again she didn't want to go anywhere or see anyone.

My stammering became much worse as time went by. The following spring, March, I believe, she decided that what I needed was complete isolation, that this might cure my stammer.

RANGE LAKE: A CURE FOR STAMMERING

My mother decided to cure my stammering. I was to stay at the cottage on Range Lake (my father was caretaker of the cottage) for about a week, by myself. I was to have no books to read. I guess I was supposed to meditate on my sins, or something! She bundled me up with food and blankets and had my father take me in by sleigh. My father was against the idea.

The lake is about two or three miles through wilderness from our farm. The snow was still two or three feet deep. I took my little hand sleigh so I could bring fire wood to the cottage. I was eleven years old, so this sounded like an exciting adventure. The first couple of days were fun. I explored the cottage and surrounding area, although the snow was quite deep and unbroken. I found some papers and magazines to read, but the nights and the darkness were frightening. I could hear packs of wolves howling in the distance, and suddenly the adventure didn't seem so exciting.

The second night, I wasn't feeling too well. My throat and eyes were burning and I felt nauseous. Did I mention that I was quite frequently ill with fever, nausea and headaches as a child? Now a wind storm was coming up, blowing across the lake. The cottage was built on a high promontory of rock, and although it was well secured (as a child, I didn't know this) a strong wind would cause it to shake and creak. With every strong gust, it felt as if the cottage would blow right off the rock and into the lake. And it was cold. The cottage hadn't been built for winter use. I was afraid to keep the fire going in the heater, for fear sparks could start a roof fire. I was terrified to stay in the cottage. There was another log cabin nearby, built low to the ground. I didn't have a key, but I decided I would be safer there. I took my lantern and plowed my way through the snow. The only way to get in the cabin was to break a window. I was afraid to build a fire in the heater there, because sometimes the chimney would be blocked to keep birds out. I huddled in blankets until morning.

The wind had died down by morning, and the sun was shining, but I was so cold and feeling really ill. I just wanted to go home! I packed up my little sleigh and began the long trek back. Although a trail had been broken with our trip in, the snow was still deep and wet. My feet were soon soaked and felt frozen. I hadn't gone far when I began to feel dizzy and threw up. Finally, I abandoned the sleigh. I didn't have enough strength to pull it. I would have to stop and rest every few feet. I didn't think I was going to make it home, and I kept thinking about the wolves I had heard howling.

My father was out doing farm chores and he saw me coming across the field. He came to meet me and helped me home. I remember he was angry, not at me, at my mother, and my mother was quite subdued. I was ill with a fever for several days. It hadn't helped my stammering, if anything, it had made it worse! I know I had nightmares for some time after that experience.

I have since often wondered why my mother couldn't see the dangers I was being placed in, especially after losing two children already. And also why wasn't my father more assertive?

Range Lake (photo from 1999)

TWIN BOYS

When I was about twelve years old, my mother decided to take in and raise six month old twin boys. They had been born to a single mother and no-one wanted them. They were neglected and not in very good health. I understand their grandfather was the father and that would account for the one child being mentally retarded. Of course my mother didn't know this at the time.

The only reason she did this, and these are her own words, is that she hoped "God would forgive her, for being so angry with Him for taking away her two children."

My parents really couldn't afford to take care of two more children. It stretched their resources to the limit. I'm not certain my father wanted to do this, but as I said before, my mother could be very determined when she wanted something.

Perhaps she thought the boys would be a great help on the farm when they were older. This didn't happen. The one boy, being mentally retarded, required a great deal of care, and the other was no help at all and was in fact a financial drain, even when he should have been out on his own.

Our new family, from left to right: myself, Minnie, Peter, Charles, Esther, and Paul

45

CHURCH AND CATECHISM

Understandably, we didn't get out to church very often, although my mother was very religious. On Sunday there were prayers and a reading from the Bible.

It was an occasion when we did get to church. We dressed in our best and had to be on our best behavior. Our pew was beside one of the windows, which was quite often open. Outside was a tree, with a robin's nest. I could watch the baby robins from our pew. My mother would have to remind me to kneel for prayers or stand for the hymns.

When I was twelve years old, my mother decided I was to be confirmed in the church. The ceremony was to be held in the fall. For two months, almost every Sunday, I had to walk the eight miles to church, for the 10 am lessons. Some Sundays my parents would attend the services and I would get a ride. Coming home, I would sometimes get a ride part way with my uncle.

I was a teenager now. I was becoming lonelier, and becoming increasingly unhappy with the isolation and the stifling conditions under which we were living. We were going to church occasionally and I was attending the catechism classes.

When I went by myself I had to pass my Aunt Amelia's house. Elizabeth was taking the same classes and we would walk together. She would regale me with stories of the fun she had at school with her friends.

I knew there was a bigger world out there, and I wanted to be part of it. Elizabeth would tell me of some dance or wedding they were going to attend, and I would ask my mother if we could go also. She would tell me we were too busy to take time to go to these affairs.

We had a radio now, left behind by the owner of the cottage at Range Lake. We listened to the country and western singers early in the morning, and my mother became addicted to some of the "Soaps." Each one was on about fifteen minutes only. Her favorites were "Ma Perkins" and "Pepper Young's family." There would be news in the evening, a couple of comedy shows a week, and a religious program on Sunday. We had to use the radio sparingly because it was battery operated and batteries were expensive.

I had no new clothing, except shoes and boots. I was still wearing dresses sent by the Hollands. One Sunday we had stopped for lunch at Aunt Amelia's and my Uncle Russell, who had never been known for his tact, criticized my outfit and my mother for trying to make me look like an "old woman". I refused to wear that particular dress again.

My mother was becoming frustrated with me because, unlike Esther who was stoic and seemingly quite content with being told what to do and how to do it, I was becoming increasingly unhappy and dissatisfied with my life.

Me at Confirmation

GROWING UP QUICKLY

As a teenager, I wanted a guitar because we listened to a lot of country and western singers on the radio. My dad said he would give me a penny for every ten potato bugs I picked off the potato plants. There were a lot of potato bugs, but I don't know if I earned enough from that. I had some other money, there was other money given to me, and I was able to get my first guitar at the cost of nine whole dollars. I loved that guitar. I learned how to do the chords. I wasn't very good at it, but it didn't last very long.

When hunting season for deer and moose opened in the fall, my father would act as guide for hunters who came from as far away as Ottawa. One group came from Shawville. One of the men, almost as old as my father, would single me out and talk to me, asking me about myself and telling me how pretty I was. He came several times and continued to visit long after hunting season was over. My mother began to extol his virtues. He owned a very large farm, was quite wealthy, and was good looking. He would make a very good "catch" for me. I told her I was afraid of him.

When he began to talk openly of marriage, it was decided I should spend a couple of weeks at his place first to get used to the idea. His mother lived with him and would act as chaperone. I was sixteen!!

I was terrified. I told my mother I didn't want to go, but she said I should give it a try for a couple of weeks. The house was quite grand, compared to what I was used to, but his mother was anything but friendly. She was fierce and stern, never smiled, and dressed in black, with her hair pulled back in a tight knot. She was rigid and harsh. Everything had to be done her way. Not even a tea towel could be folded incorrectly. No little sixteen year old upstart was going to come into her house and change anything.

Every evening, after supper, Fred, his name was Fred, would drink until bedtime. I believe all this man wanted was a wife to help his mother take care of the house and garden, someone young and strong. I don't think he had ever been married before. Probably because his mother had scared them all off!

I couldn't sleep at night. I was so frightened. I knew I couldn't marry this man, but I was afraid my mother would insist. After three days I decided to run away. I had a few dollars my father had slipped me "just in case I needed anything," but I knew it wasn't enough to get me to Ottawa. I had noticed there was some money kept in a tin on a shelf – I had found it because I thought it was a tea tin. Late in the night, I gathered together my few things, took about thirty dollars from the tin and walked out to the highway. The farm wasn't too far from the highway. I hitched a ride with a truck driver. I was lucky, he was going to Ottawa! When the truck driver asked where I was going, I said I didn't know. I needed to find some place to stay. He was very kind and dropped me off at the YWCA.

In hindsight, my mother probably would never have forced me to marry this man, and I doubt my father would have allowed it, but I was young, frightened, and not thinking too clearly.

49

OTTAWA YEARS

The people at the YWCA were very kind and helpful. I was shown how to find work through the want ads in the paper, and they actually helped me find a job with a Jewish family as a girl of all work. I wrote my parents, letting them know I was alright and told them I would pay back the money I had stolen. I didn't tell them where I was living.

A few months later, I followed up an ad in the paper for a nursemaid and was accepted. I had enough experience helping with the twin boys, so I knew pretty well what I was doing. The little boy I was to look after was two years old. He was a very quiet child, easy to look after. My duties were to see to his meals, keep him and his rooms clean, play with him, and take him to the park. His father worked for the French Embassy. They had a housekeeper-cook and daily cleaning help.

The house was large and beautiful. I had my own suite of rooms. I must have done something right! I was with them for over two and a half years.

This again was a very lonely time for me. Living in a large city after growing up in almost total isolation on a primitive farm, was like being transplanted to an alien planet. I knew nothing about city life. I had no friends. I met some of the other nursemaids in the park, but I had nothing in common with them. I couldn't converse with them, because most of the time I didn't know what they were talking about! So I watched and listened and learned.

I continued my self-education as best I could. I still hadn't made any friends, except for the housekeeper-cook. I guess I had been a "loner" for too long. Anyway, one doesn't get to meet too many people in my line of work.

The people I worked for were very nice, warm and friendly. The lady I worked for insisted on calling me Madeline, and I guess it stuck. I have never been called Magdalene. They would invite me to join them in the evenings when they were home, although I felt very shy and inadequate, being aware of my lack of education and my ignorance.

I discovered LIBRARIES! Here again, I didn't know what I wanted to read, or even what I could read. I would take out as many books at random as I was allowed. My reading skills were not great, and I found the books would pose more questions than I could find answers for.

Someone mentioned they were taking classes at night school. I enrolled in high school night classes, but soon found it was beyond me because I didn't have even the basics in most of the subjects. There was no one to give me any help, and the instructor was indifferent. His time was taken up with the smarter students. So, my spare time was spent reading, listening and learning as much as I could on my own.

I went to the odd movie on my time off. I didn't have much money to spare, my wardrobe was in a deplorable state, and I was paying back the money I had taken.

RETURN TO OTTER LAKE

For the first year I didn't let my parents know where I was in Ottawa. Just that I was alright. When I sent the last of the money I had taken, I sent my address as well. The first letter I received from my mother, she was very angry. She said I had humiliated her and my father, that Fred had been furious with them, and that I had broken one of God's Ten Commandments, stealing, and I would surely be punished for that transgression. (She might have been right in that!)

I was about eighteen and a half when I became very ill with chicken pox and measles at the same time. My employers had to find another nursemaid, and when it became apparent I was going to take several weeks to fully recover, I reluctantly contacted my parents and asked if I could come home. My mother made arrangements for someone to come and bring me home. I believe she thought I had had enough of city life and I was home to stay.

My father welcomed me back with open arms. He was so pleased to see me again. I returned in late fall, and that winter I had to help my father cut and haul logs in the bush. I enjoyed working with my father, and I know he enjoyed having me there with him. We spent many happy hours together while I told him about my adventures in the big city. At break and lunch time, we would build a fire to thaw our frozen sandwiches and melt snow water in a tin can to make tea. I guess I had never been too strong, and I found the hard work in the freezing cold too much for me. I was losing a lot of weight and frequently coming down with colds.

In the spring, I decided to return to Ottawa once again. When I went back to Ottawa, I should have gone back to being a nursemaid, but I wanted to try something different. I answered an ad for an apprentice in a hair dressing salon. They were supposed to teach me the skills of cutting and styling hair. At the end of three months, I was still sweeping floors and cleaning basins, and I was being paid such a low salary, I didn't always have enough money for food.

One Sunday I was visiting my Aunt Amelia, who worked in Ottawa in the winter. I met my cousin Emmy from Kapuskasing. She and her brother had been visiting and were driving back to Kapuskasing. She suggested I should go back with them. A new adventure for me!

I gave in my notice at the beauty shop and went back with them. My cousin, Arnold, gave me a job working in his taxi company, but I didn't like the work and I didn't like Kapuskasing, so once again I headed back to Ottawa. Unfortunately, I didn't have enough funds to get farther than Sudbury. I had to stop there, taking a job at a diner until I had saved enough money to carry on.

In Sudbury I met Erol. I was very young and very naive. Erol was so charming and handsome and I just fell madly in love with him – or maybe it wasn't love, maybe he just charmed me? We went for long walks, we would stop for coffee, and we'd just talk. He was my first boyfriend, and he was really, really charming. We married and we lived in Sudbury for quite a few years. And there begins a new chapter in my life.

With a horse on the farm

EPILOGUE

Magdalene's adult life could be divided into two segments: The Hembroff years and the Aitken years.

Magdalene married Erol Hembroff, a blind young man who ran a newsstand in Sudbury. They had four children together, one of whom was sadly adopted out. Their children were Christine, Thomas, Donald, and Helaine (adopted out and named Sharon). They also raised a foster child as their own, Judith Alexine.

The family moved several times: Sudbury, returning to Otter Lake, then Ottawa, Toronto and Vancouver. The marriage ended when the children were in their teens.

In 1966 Magdalene met Robert Aitken and eventually married him, having one child, Katie. The new family lived in North Delta, BC, near Vancouver, then in Whitehorse, Yukon. After Robert retired, they moved to Vancouver Island, and then back to Whitehorse.

Charles and Minnie stayed on the Otter Lake farm the rest of their lives. After Magdalene left home, Charles and Minnie spent over 20 years building a 'dream house' for Minnie. It was a two-story stone house with indoor plumbing from Zimmerling Lake. Unfortunately the home was destroyed in a fire in 1975.

After the fire, Minnie and Charles moved to a small house in Otter Lake, too old to rebuild the house and too old to continue living on the farm. Esther remained at home with them and stayed on in the house after their deaths, until she had to be moved to a long term care facility. Charles passed away in 1980 at age 91 and Minnie passed away in 1988 at age 92.

I am so very proud of my children and grandchildren. You are all so very strong, kind and generous. Beautiful people!

The author in 2010